ONE HAND CLAPPING

ZEN STORIES FOR ALL AGES

Selected, adapted, and retold by

Rafe Martin
and
Manuela Soares

Illustrations by Junko Morimoto

RIZZOLI
NEW YORK

Table of Contents

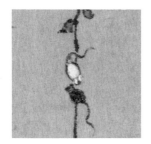

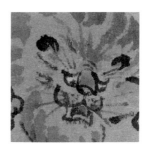

INTRODUCTION

Among the sixteen kinds of meditation, the baby's practice is the best.

YUAN-WU

How delightful it is
To play with the children
The whole spring day,
When the mist is gone!

RYOKAN
(from *Dewdrops on the Lotus,* Jakob Fischer)

The stories in this collection are all from or about Zen, the spiritual tradition which began twenty-five hundred years ago in India with the life and experience of the Buddha. "Zen" is a Japanese word. It comes from the Sanskrit word "dhyana," and the Chinese word "ch'an," both of which mean "meditation." In Zen meditation, or *zazen,* a Zen student learns to let his or her mind rest at ease, beyond all limiting thought forms. In this freedom of mind, we can realize our true nature, our oneness with everyone and everything.

Who was the Buddha? He was a prince born in the sixth century B.C., and the name his parents actually gave him was Siddhartha. It was a beautiful name for, in Sanskrit, Siddhartha means "every wish fulfilled." As a young man Prince Siddhartha was moved by the sufferings of others. Even the sufferings of birds and animals caused him concern. "That's good," thought his father, "when he becomes king he'll care about his subjects." But Siddhartha wanted to do more than be a king. One day, when he was twenty-nine years old, he suddenly left the wealth of his father's palace and, all alone, set out to find a way to free himself, and all living beings, from the sufferings of old age, sickness, change, and death.

One morning, after six years of meditation in the forests and mountains, just as he glanced up at the morning star, he suddenly experienced Enlightenment. In a flash he saw how every plant, tree, bug, stone, animal, person, and star is itself the entire Universe and is entirely Perfect just as it is, free from all limitation or suffering. He saw clearly, too, how our clouded thinking makes it seem and feel quite otherwise. After that he was known as the Buddha, which means "the Awakened One," and he dedicated every day of his life to joyfully helping others.

Most of the stories in this collection, however, are not about the Buddha himself. Rather, they come from the lives of the Zen masters of China and Japan who helped pass on the Buddha's teachings to us today. Others are stories that show the wisdom, directness, and spontaneity for which Zen is known. All these stories can help us see past our seeming differences into what is the same for all of us, for everyone.

Beside teaching their students to meditate, Zen masters delight in using the ordinary events of life as ways of awakening the Mind. There are kinds of Zen stories which show this taking place and which can initiate a search for this Awakened Mind in ourselves. They are called *koans*. Zen Master Hakuin's question—What is the sound of one hand?—is a very direct kind of koan. To resolve a koan, one must learn to face it completely, with one's whole being, and not just think about it. Concentrating on a koan in a seated meditation or zazen, a Zen student may awaken to an awareness of True Mind in which each thing is fully itself and is also completely interwoven with all other things.

In folktales from around the world this kind of awareness can be represented as a realm in which all things are alive and can talk. In folktales and fairy tales ravens, bees, and ants talk; clods of earth, raindrops, pebbles, and trees converse freely. We might discover that during the depths of the night the stars can answer the flowing streams. In such folk stories the universe itself is revealed to be one great ongoing conversation in which everyone and everything participates equally. Traditional folktales can point us towards this ancient truth. Zen folktales called koans ask us to experience it ourselves.

Having a "Zen mind" or a "beginner's mind," that is, a mind that is open and alert without limitations or prejudice, is a way we can begin this process of awakening the Mind. Zen mind and the mind of a child are alike. Both can receive impressions and experiences freshly, without unnecessary judgments. Both can respond unself-consciously to the daily wonders of life itself. We might say that Zen masters and children have a lot in common.

The Japanese Zen monk Ryokan comes to mind. Though he spent much of his later life alone in a mountain hermitage doing zazen, writing poetry, and keeping up with simple chores like gathering herbs and firewood, he also loved to join in the games of the village children. Their minds and his were in natural harmony, peacefully at one with each other and with the world around them.

When Zen Master Dogen, one of the truly towering figures of Japanese Zen, was asked what he brought back from his three years of intense spiritual training in China he answered simply, "a tender-heart." The stories in this collection are for the tender heart that children and adults naturally share. May you enjoy reading, telling, and sharing these—and other—Zen stories. The seeds they plant can grow, in time, into a rich harvest indeed.

—Rafe Martin

EDITOR'S NOTE

The stories in this collection are meant for parents and children to share, though they can also be enjoyed by solitary readers. They were selected to spark discussion and contemplation as well as to amuse and delight.

These stories are not always easy to understand—their simplicity can be deceiving. In practicing Zen, students often contemplate a particular *koan* (a story or question) for a very long time, gaining new insights and a deeper understanding. The stories and koans presented here can go beyond words—pointing towards a new way of looking at the world. With this in mind, it is good to remember that there is no right or wrong way to interpret these tales, there are no good or bad questions, and no definitive answers.

Read alone or together, these stories are meant to evoke questions, to elicit wonder and amusement, and encourage contemplation. These stories can be an adventure for children and adults—an exploration of their meaning a journey taken together. But they might also show that adults don't have all the answers—and children aren't the only ones with questions.

—Manuela Soares

THE TIGERS AND THE STRAWBERRY

The Buddha told this story: **A** man was walking across a field when he saw a tiger. He fled, but the tiger ran after him. Coming to the edge of a cliff, he spied the root of a wild vine. Grabbing on to it, he swung himself down over the edge, out of reach of the tiger. He was safe!

The tiger came to the edge and sniffed at him from above. Trembling, the man looked down and saw another ferocious tiger prowling below. Only the thin vine held him.

Two mice, one white and one black, scurried out of a nearby nest in the cliff and began gnawing at the vine. As they chewed, the man saw a luscious strawberry on a nearby ledge. Grasping the vine with one hand, he plucked the strawberry with the other.

Ah, how sweet it tasted!

Learning to Be Silent

There once were four young men who practiced Zen together. One day, they decided to spend seven days of *zazen* meditation in complete silence.

Everything started off well. But, when evening came at the end of the first day, the oil lamps became dimmer and dimmer. One of them couldn't help saying, "We should fix those lamps."

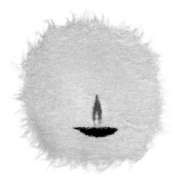

Another, surprised to hear the first one speak, said, "Shhhhh. We're not supposed to say a word!"

"You two really goofed. Why did you talk?" asked a third.

"Well, it looks like I'm the only one who hasn't broken down and said anything," announced the fourth.

They looked at one another and began to laugh. All had been equally foolish! They decided they'd have to try again. But this time they would remain really alert.

THE ZEN MASTER AND THE SAMURAI

Once a samurai came before Zen Master Hakuin.

"You're supposed to be a great Zen master," he said. "So I want you to tell me the truth about heaven and hell. Do they really exist?"

Without a moment's hesitation Hakuin responded, "What, even such an ugly and untalented man as you can become a samurai? Amazing!"

Immediately the proud samurai became angry and drew his sword. "I'll kill you!" he roared.

Fearlessly Hakuin said, "This is hell."

The samurai paused and grew thoughtful. His face softened from its angry scowl. Sheathing his sword he put his hands together palm to palm and bowed before Hakuin.

"And this," said Hakuin, just as calmly, "is heaven."

"COME BODHISATTVAS, EAT ALL YOU WANT!"

Long ago in China there lived a Zen master named Chin Niu. Hundreds of novices came to his temple to be trained in Zen. Many came to attain peace of mind, but many also came because they had heard that no one ever went hungry there.

Every morning they sat in Zen meditation. Afterwards, some swept out the meditation hall, while others gathered wood, and still others drew water from the well or worked in the garden. Everyone had a job to do.

One morning another novice joined the group. "I was told that I should never be hungry here," he said. Many laughed for they, too, had initially come to Chin Niu for the same reason.

When the bell tolled for lunch they all walked silently to the dining room. They recited the mealtime chants, thanking all those whose hard work had provided the meal, and the many beings — even the grains and the vegetables — for their sharing of life.

A jolly voice called out, "Come Bodhisattvas! Eat all you want, as much as you like!" In the doorway stood an old monk holding a big bowl of rice. Doing a little dance for joy, he began serving everyone all by himself!

The newcomer was astonished to learn that the old monk was none other than Chin Niu himself, and that every day the great teacher personally cooked for and served his hundreds of disciples.

The Cherry Blossoms

A nun, Rengetsu by name, was on a pilgrimage when she stopped in a small town seeking shelter for the night. It had been a long and difficult journey and she was very tired. She went from door to door asking for a place to stay, but no one would let her in.

It was sunset now and getting darker by the minute, so she finally just made her bed for the night in a field under a cherry tree. In the middle of the night she awoke to find the cherry tree in full blossom beneath a beautiful silvery moon. The sight was breathtaking! Awed by this unexpected beauty, she turned toward the village, bowed, and uttered this little prayer of thanks:

*Through their
kindness in refusing
me lodging,*

*I found myself
beneath the
beautiful blossoms*

*on the night of the
misty moon.*

THE THREE ANSWERS

One day an emperor decided that if he knew the answers to three questions, he would always know what to do, no matter what. So he made an announcement throughout his kingdom that if anyone could answer his three questions, he would give them a big reward.

These were the questions:

> When is the best time to do things?
> Who are the most important people?
> What is the most important thing?

The emperor received many answers, but none satisfied him. Finally he decided to travel up the mountain to visit a hermit who lived at the top. Perhaps he would know the answers.

When he reached the hermit, he asked his three questions. The hermit, who was digging in his garden, listened attentively and then returned to his digging without saying a word. As the hermit continued digging, the emperor noticed how tired the old man seemed. "Here," he said, "give me the spade. I'll dig and you can rest for a while." So the hermit rested while the emperor dug.

After digging for several hours, the emperor was

very tired. He put down the spade and said, "If you can't answer my questions, that's all right. Just tell me and I'll take my leave."

"Do you hear someone running?" asked the hermit suddenly, pointing to the edge of the woods. And sure enough, a man came tumbling out of the woods, clutching his stomach. He collapsed as the hermit and the emperor reached him. Opening the man's shirt, they saw that he had a deep cut. The emperor cleaned the wound, using his own shirt to bind it. Regaining consciousness, the man asked for water. The emperor hurried to a nearby stream and brought him some. The man drank gratefully, then slept.

The hermit and the emperor carried the man into the hut and lay him on the hermit's bed. By this time, the emperor, too, was exhausted and he soon fell asleep.

The next morning when the emperor awoke, he saw the wounded man standing there, staring down at him. "Forgive me," the man whispered. "Forgive you?" said the emperor, sitting up, wide awake. "What have you done that needs my forgiveness?"

"You do not know me your majesty, but I have thought of you as my sworn enemy. During the last war you killed my brother and took away my lands. So I swore vengeance and vowed to kill you. And, indeed, yesterday I was lying in ambush, waiting for you to come back down the mountain so that I could kill you. I waited a long time, but, for some reason, you didn't return. So I left my hiding place to find you. Instead, your attendants found me and, recognizing me, attacked, giving me a painful wound. I fled but, if you hadn't helped me when you did, I surely would have died. I had planned to kill you. Instead you saved my life! I am ashamed and very grateful. Please forgive me."

The emperor was astonished. "I am glad," he said, "that your hatred has ended. I am sorry, too, now that I have heard your story, for the pain I have clearly caused you. War is terrible. I forgive you and I restore your lands. Let us be friends from this time on." After instructing his attendants to take the man safely home, the emperor turned once again to the hermit. "I must leave now," he said. "I shall travel everywhere seeking the answers to my three questions. I hope someday I can find them. Farewell."

The hermit laughed and said, "Your questions are already answered, your majesty."

"What do you mean?" exclaimed the emperor in surprise.

The hermit explained. "If you had not helped me dig my garden yesterday, delaying your return, you would have been attacked on your way home. Therefore, the most important time for you was the time you were digging in my garden. The most important person was myself, the person you were with, and the most important pursuit was simply to help me.

"Later, when the wounded man came, the most important time was the time you spent tending his wound, for otherwise he would have died and you would have lost forever the opportunity for forgiveness and friendship. At that moment he was the most important person and the most important pursuit was tending his wound.

"The present moment is the only moment," said the hermit. "The most important person is always the person you are with. And the most important pursuit is making the person standing at your side happy. What could be simpler or more important?"

The emperor bowed in gratitude to the old hermit and left in peace.

IKKYU'S POISON

W hen Zen Master Ikkyu was still a child, he began to study Zen in a monastery. Ikkyu's master had a jar of candy that he was particularly fond of and, to keep the novices from eating it, he told them that the jar was filled with poison. Ikkyu, however, was not fooled. One day he opened the jar and ate some of the delicious candy. It was so good he shared it with the other novices. They all enjoyed the candy very much and ate every last piece. Ikkyu then dropped the jar and broke it.

When the master returned, Ikkyu went to him and said, "Master, I dropped your favorite jar and broke it."

"Well" said the master, "all things must pass. It's good you told me. Where is the poison that was inside?"

"Oh Master," said Ikkyu, "when the jar broke I felt so bad about it that I ate the poison. I thought it a fitting punishment. But strangely, nothing has happened to me."

The master looked suspiciously at Ikkyu, but the boy just stood there quietly. "Er, yes, hummph," said the master. "Very strange. You are a lucky child, after all." And, still somewhat confused, he let Ikkyu go.

The Fish in the Sea

nce upon a time a baby fish asked an older, larger fish about the sea.

"What is the sea?" he asked. "I keep hearing about it, but I don't know what it is."

"Why the sea is all around you, little one," said the grown-up fish.

"If that's so, why can't I see it?" asked the young fish.

"Because it is *everywhere*. It surrounds you. It's inside and outside you. You were born in the sea and you will die in the sea. What's more, you yourself are the life of the sea. When you swim you reveal its presence. It's just because it's so close to you that it's very hard to see. But don't worry, it's here."

RYOKAN AND THE PERSIMMONS

One fine autumn afternoon, Ryokan, the famous Zen monk and poet, was passing through a village on the way back to his little hut in the mountains when he heard a shout for help. Turning towards the cry, he discovered a boy clinging to the topmost branches of a persimmon tree. Unable to get down and afraid of falling, the boy was calling for help.

Putting down his staff and his bowl, Ryokan called out, "Coming, boy. Just hold on. I'll get you down."

Climbing the tree he reached the boy and helped him to safety. "I'll get some of the persimmons that you were trying to reach," Ryokan said. "I'll get as many as you can eat. Just wait here." Then back he went up into the tree, higher and higher. At last, perched at the very tip-top, Ryokan very carefully reached out, for balancing at the top of that tree wasn't easy, and plucked a persimmon.

"I'd better taste it," he thought. "Why pick them if they're not yet ripe?" So he took a bite. Oh, but it was sweet! So he ate it. The tree swayed in the wind, the clouds floated overhead.

The warm
autumn sun
shone down.
Ryokan picked
another. He took a bite.
Ummm sweet! How sweet!
So he ate that one, too. And
another and another.

Ryokan forgot about everything.
Swaying up in the top of that tree,
eating those sweet persimmons, his delight
was boundless.

Then he heard a voice calling. Who could it be? He
looked down and remembered the boy! Lost in rapture,
Ryokan had forgotten all about him! "Oh! How forgetful!"
he exclaimed. "My apologies," he called down to the boy.
"Here come your persimmons. The very best, ripe and sweet.
All for you. Catch!" Then one by one he picked the ripe
persimmons and dropped them down to the waiting child.

THE ART OF SWORDSMANSHIP

O nce a young man named Manjuro sought out the greatest sword-master in the country, a man named Banzo, wanting to become his student.

"How long," Manjuro asked, "will it take me to become a master swordsman?"

Banzo replied, "Your entire life."

"I can't wait that long," said Manjuro. "What if I become your devoted servant, how long then?"

"Maybe ten years," said Banzo.

"That's still too long," said Manjuro. "What if I work even harder, day and night? How long then?"

"Thirty years, then," Banzo said.

"Thirty years!" exclaimed Manjuro. "First you tell me ten, and then thirty. How can that be?"

"A man in such a hurry seldom learns quickly," said Banzo.

Understanding that he was being reprimanded for impatience, Manjuro agreed to become Banzo's servant. "However long it takes," he vowed, "I will become a great swordsman!"

But to his dismay, for the first year he did nothing but sweep and clean, chop wood, wash dishes, cook, carry water, and other such household tasks. He never got a

chance to even look at a sword, much less handle one! "I will be patient," Manjuro said to himself. "Surely Banzo is just testing my determination." But the second year was the same as the first. As was the third. Time went on but Manjuro received no training in swordsmanship.

Finally Manjuro became quite upset. "I'd better leave," he thought. "I'm not learning a thing and time is going by." A short time later, while Manjuro was working in the garden, Banzo quietly approached him and thwacked him with a wooden sword. Whack! The next day Banzo again surprised Manjuro and whack! hit him again. Soon, Manjuro became alert at all times — cooking, cleaning, chopping wood — for, whack! he never knew when Banzo might strike again with the blunt wooden sword.

Gradually, something extraordinary began to happen.

As the sword descended, Manjuro instantly and instinctively blocked the oncoming blow with a pot lid, a broom, or a piece of wood. Sharpened naturally by the constant and unexpected attacks of Banzo, Manjuro had become a talented swordsman! No one could overcome him now — not even the great swordsman Banzo himself.

And so, Manjuro went on to become even greater than his teacher.

MOUNTAINS AND RIVERS

n old woman was talking to her grandson. She said:

"Before I grasped Zen, the mountains were only mountains and the rivers were only rivers. When I got into Zen, the mountains were no longer mountains and the rivers were no longer rivers. But when I understood Zen, the mountains were mountains and the rivers were rivers."

"Granny," said the little boy.

"Yes, grandson," she answered.

"The river's right here and it's a hot day. Can't we go swimming?" he asked.

"Of course," she laughed, "just jump right in!"

THE LION
AND
THE TIGER

A zoo once had a famous tiger. One day the tiger died. Since it was very expensive to replace the tiger, the zoo hired a beggar to dress up in a tiger skin during zoo hours, sit in the cage, and pretend to be the tiger. This actually worked quite well. The people believed the famous tiger was still there, and the beggar had a home.

One day two men began arguing in front of the tiger cage.

"The tiger is the strongest of animals," said one of the men. "Its roar is the mightiest. It's the most ferocious of beasts, and this one is a terrific specimen."

"Nonsense," replied the other man. He pointed to the lion in the next cage. "Everyone knows that the lion is the king of the beasts. When he roars, everyone trembles! And just look at this one here—he's magnificent!"

The men continued to quarrel until finally they persuaded the zookeeper to let the two animals fight each other to see which was actually the mightiest. They promised to pay the zookeeper if either animal was killed.

Hearing this, the "tiger" was terrified, but before he could do anything, the cage door opened and in bounded the lion.

A crowd gathered as the roaring lion furiously chased the tiger all around the cage, finally pouncing on him. The tiger trembled with fear.

"This is the end," thought the poor tiger. "I am about to be eaten by a lion."

But then the lion whispered softly in his ear, "Not to worry. I'm the same as you!"

BABY SNAKE
IN A CUP

One evening, a man was invited to the home of a friend. As he was about to drink a cup of tea that was offered to him, he thought he saw a baby snake in the cup! He did not want to embarrass his hostess, so he gathered all of his courage and swallowed the tea in one gulp.

When the man returned home later that night, he began to feel severe pains in his stomach. By the next day the pains had grown worse. He consulted several doctors and tried many cures, but none worked. The man, now seriously ill, thought he was about to die.

Hearing of his condition, his friend invited him to visit her again. Sitting in the same place, he accepted another cup of tea. As the sick man lifted his cup to drink, he suddenly saw the snake again! This time he had to speak up, so he drew his hostess's attention to it. Without a word she pointed to the ceiling above her guest. He looked up. There, just above him, hanging from a beam, was a length of rope. The sick man realized all at once that what he had thought was a baby snake was simply the reflection of the rope! The two friends looked at each other and laughed. The pain of the sick man vanished instantly and he recovered perfect health.

SAIGYO AT THE FERRY

Saigyo, a 12th-century haiku poet and Buddhist priest of Japan, was traveling with his disciple, Saio. Each morning they set out at sunrise and, at evening, they would stop at an inn or a temple or a farmer's house or the home of a poet and spend the night. When there was no place nearby they slept outdoors beneath the stars.

The two travelers came to the Tenryu River and boarded the ferry to cross. Just as the ferry was about to leave, a samurai came running up, shouting, "Stop! Wait!"

The boatman bowed to the samurai. "As you can see, the boat is already full," he said quite humbly. "Will you please wait for the next one?"

"Impossible!" roared the samurai. "Me wait? Never! Get someone else off the boat. Hey you," he shouted at Saigyo. "You leave!"

Saigyo just sat there and looked out over the water. It was as if he had not heard the order at all. Then the samurai charged at Saigyo and struck him on the forehead with a large folded fan. Blood gushed from the cut but Saigyo seemed unmoved. Saio, who knew how strong his master was and who also knew that Saigyo had once himself been a famous samurai, sat in expectation. Any minute now Saigyo would certainly stand up and throw the samurai overboard. But Saigyo did nothing of the sort. Instead he simply rose and got off the boat silently,

followed by the unhappy and disappointed Saio. With a triumphant sneer the samurai got on board and the boat left the shore.

"Why didn't you say anything when he treated you like that?" asked Saio. "Aren't you angry with him?"

"No," answered Saigyo.

"But why?" demanded Saio in frustration.

"I am a monk," answered Saigyo.

"But you can knock down three or four of him," said Saio.

"Don't be silly," said Saigyo. "What would that prove?"

"But I was so disappointed," exclaimed Saio, near tears. "Everybody was laughing at us."

"Must I be foolish just because others are?"

"Then you are a coward," pronounced Saio.

"Really, don't be silly. Monks have to endure such trifles. This is the way I am determined to train myself," said Saigyo. "If you cannot do it just say so and I'll travel on alone."

"Anyone would say that it was right to beat such an intolerable fellow," insisted Saio.

The master was silent. When the next boat came he boarded it. Saio did not. "Good-bye Saio," said the master as he waved to his disciple. Slowly the boat headed out from shore.

Saio let him go without a word.
It took him a long time before he
realized his mistake and regretted
parting with his master.

Saigyo continued his journey. He
felt as if he had nothing to fear
in this world.

BECOMING BUDDHA

Ma-tsu sat in meditation for long periods every day outside his little hut. His Zen master, Haui-jang, watched him one day and thought, "He will become a very worthy person. Still, right now he is stuck and needs some help."

"Noble one," he asked, "what are you trying to get by sitting in meditation?"

"I am trying to become a Buddha," Ma-tsu replied with conviction.

Hearing this, Haui-jang picked up a rough clay tile that had fallen from the temple roof and began rubbing it against a rock.

"What are you doing, Master?" asked Ma-tsu.

"I am polishing this rough tile to make it a precious jewel," the master replied.

"How can a roof tile ever become a jewel?" asked Ma-tsu.

"How can you become a Buddha through Zen meditation," Haui-jang replied, "if you weren't already a Buddha to begin with? Walking, standing, lying down, sitting — who are you in each of these activities? Real Zen is not confined to sitting. Live Buddhas are not just found in the lotus posture."

Hearing this, Ma-tsu felt as refreshed as if he had just drunk the most delicious drink.

THE SOUND OF A SINGLE HAND

The great Zen master, Hakuin, who lived in 18th-century Japan, used to hold up his hand before his students and say, "Listen to the sound of a single hand."

Or he would ask, "What is the sound of a single hand?"

In the depths of the innermost self, more remote than the farthest mountain, and closer than close,

Lies the secret house of the sound of one hand. Enter!

BODHIDHARMA AND THE CHILDREN

The Great Teacher, Bodhidharma, was the one who brought Zen from India to China long, long ago. It was said that when he was young he had been a royal prince. But one day he left home to seek the Truth. He disappeared and no one knew where to find him.

One day some children were exploring a cave in the mountains. In the back of the cave they saw something strange. It looked like a bear, but perhaps it was just a pile of boulders. It was too dark to tell. Whatever it was it didn't move so, after a time, they lost some of their fear. "Let's get closer," they whispered to one another, "and see if we can find out what it really is."

They stepped forward. Closer, closer. They saw some small stones lying on the cave floor. Each child bent down and picked one up. They looked at each other, then, all together, they threw the stones at the silent form and then ran to a safe distance to watch. The rocks hit with a thud. The children watched in expectation. Slowly the still figure began to move. It rocked from side to side and began to roar — with laughter! Those rocks had hit Bodhidharma himself, who had been silently meditating in the back of the cave! The instant those rocks hit his doubts fell away and he realized Enlightenment!

A Silver Cat

Once a famous poet who had trained for a long time in Zen was invited to come speak with the emperor. When their conversation was finished the emperor was so impressed with the man's wisdom that he gave him a gift — a statue of a cat. The statue was made of pure silver and was worth a fortune! The poet bowed to the emperor, put the statue in the sleeve of his robe, and left. He had not gotten far from the palace gates when he came upon some children who were playing with little toy animals they had made from mud and clay. The poet took the priceless silver cat from his sleeve and gave it to the children. They were delighted! Then the poet walked on in peace, a smile on his face, humming a little ancient tune to himself.

Listen! Perhaps as the wind moves through the trees today, you too will hear it!